Lumba Poetry
Waves of Change

Barb Flett

LUMBA POETRY
Waves of Change

LUMBA POETRY
Waves of Change

Copyright © Barb Flett, 2022

Published by Barb Flett, Barrhead, Canada

ISBN:
    Paperback   978-1-77354-452-6
        ebook   978-1-77354-453-3

Publication assistance by

PAGEMASTER
PUBLISHING
PageMaster.ca

DEDICATED TO MY HUSBAND

who has given me endless support and
encouragement, with a drive to never
give up on what I believe in.
Thank you
with all of my heart, body, mind and soul.
Also to my clients, family, and friends
who listened to me!

Words to the Reader

Because today's world is changing so quickly, it's important to take some time to slow down and unwind. Put your feet up, read some poetry, get some crayons and express yourself by coloring. Transform the pictures in front of you while replenishing your body, mind, and soul. Make wellness a way of life.

LUMBA is a word of African origin related to Thanks and Praise. We must always remember to take a little time, every day, to be thankful for the blessings in our lives, no matter how small or how large they are.

May your days be filled with
> peace and calm.
May you find your purpose and
> your passion in your life
> no matter what you choose to do.
May you keep a vision within your sight
> to pull you ahead
> with every step you take.
May you find a way to always
> keep yourself well – in body, mind & spirit.
> Isn't it time to BELIEVE in
> A BETTER WAY?
May you start today!

Thank you, Lumba, Amen.

A Link of Chains

Like molecules and atoms
All drawn in lines
Creating a LINK OF CHAINS
Only some can describe

The scientists see links in ways
We will never know
But links can come in many forms

A fence can have links
To keep people out
Perhaps to keep people in
Depending on the situation

You can draw your own links
Perhaps in your mind
Using your imagination to create
Healthy ways
Believing in a structural change
Within your own self

It all starts in the mind
And some can move it about
Never disbelieve in anything
Cause and effect can use some direction

Always look at life with wonder
With a LINK OF CHAINS
Discover open possibilities

Abundance

Some of us have it
Some of us don't
You can't rely on anyone
To bring it to you
For it comes from your self
If your needs aren't met
Boy will you fret
ABUNDANCE you must search for
And know a little can be a lot
The source isn't just money
But what comes from the heart
Genuine ABUNDANCE
You will know from within

ADDICTIONS

It's a search for a feeling
One that makes us believe
We have to get it from outside us
It can be one of many things
That complicates our being
Perhaps it's
    Drugs, Alcohol, Cigarettes, Pills
    Exercise, Sports, Sex, Work, Food
That brings on the stress
And messes up the rest, deep inside
Disillusions to make us happy
Instead they usually make us feel crappy
When we constantly reach from the outside
Creating an addiction within
Ask yourself
Why do I need this fix?
Is it something good for me?
Or creating a damn that could hamper me?
What could my alternative be?
To strengthen me
From my inside, to my outside
Bringing light to me
Reserves of strength
To be found
Releasing the grip that ADDICTIONS bring

ANCHORS

I stand with my feet
Firm on the ground
My head is out of the clouds
My ANCHORS hold me down
Steadfastly letting me know
I'm where I need to be

The energies around me
Comfort my soul
For I feel so free
When my anchors secure me
To handle what life throws me
In any direction
I am prepared to catch it

Restlessness disappears
And I have no fear
When my ANCHORS
Plant me firmly on the ground
Where I need to be
So faithfully

ANGELS

Comfort me
Wrap your wings around me
Whisper encouragement in my ear
Tingle my nerves so I know you are near
Enlighten every part of me
Let me smile
And speak your truth
Ever ready to defend myself
Warm and guided all the way
Wisdom and love to always share
Knowing you're there to care
You shine your light so bright
Giving me signs to never give up
I believe in the other side
Bringing me strength
Encouragement to carry on
Silence is when I find you best
I take the time to listen to my ANGELS
Who are there to guide me
All of the time

ARE YOU AWAKE?

Are you awake?
Did you lose your faith?
Are you filled with hate?
Don't hesitate
Or it will be to late
Open your eyes
Release the lies
That flood our skies
Streaming our beings
From the outside
To the inside
Keep your eyes open wide
We have to be awake
For it could be a big quake
When heaven and earth collide
ARE YOU AWAKE?

Beliefs

From the moment
We are born in this world
BELIEFS are things
That shape our way
Good or Bad, Right or Wrong
They can't tell
The thoughts are formed and shaped
And inhabit what we concentrate on
We must trust
To find the truth
If the thoughts are not kind
They are most likely false
Love, Light and understanding
Is the key to opening closed doors
Sometimes we have to reprogram
What's been jammed
Into our minds
That sets our BELIEFS
To be free

Believe

You have to be flexible
And the timing impeccable
To reach the heights
Seeing the sights
When it all feels right
Fight for your might
Your burdens can become light
As you work with all your heart
To get to where you need to be
So you can feel free
We all have the key
To open closed doors
Never disbelieve
The impossible can become possible
If you just BELIEVE

BUTTERFLY

You've come out of your cocoon
That wrapped you in warmth
Over the cold winter
To the new season
That's born
Your beauty is radiant
Watching you
Calms me to the core
For with you
I see a chance for change
You bring hope and beauty
I know I can bring about
Transformation to my life
Just as you transformed yours
To a BUTTERFLY
From a cocoon

CHALLENGES

You can build a wall
You can break it down
To the ground
CHALLENGES will be found
Dig them up like a hound
Don't ever be bound

Treasures lie around
In places to be found
Look for the little things
That can be put together
To become something better

Keep your sights
Bright and into the light
Challenges can unfold
If you work to break them down
Letting them fall to the ground

Change your thoughts
Change your way of thinking
Change your behaviors
To change the end result
Don't let a CHALLENGE
Take a hold over you
For you are stronger
Then you believe
Find your way
To set you free
To break those CHALLENGES
To the ground

Change

CHANGE can be uncomfortable
And sometimes wonderful
It's how we take it
Be careful not to break it
For it can be good or bad
Insane or sane, kind or unkind
Just be ready to unwind
And accept the challenges it may bring
For the winds of CHANGE are unseen
So you have to be keen
Knowing you can lean
Like a willow in the wind
The roots are strong, secure to the ground
To keep you centered
To be your own mentor
Always knowing one thing for sure
That CHANGE will always be
Following us wherever we go

CLARITY

I look in the stream
There is a beam
Shining in me
So crystal clear
It makes a mirror
As my image seems so surreal
My mind becomes transparent
As the quietness I inherit
That heals every part of me
As I begin to smile
An inner smile
Deep from within
Something no one can take from me
That makes my day
As clear as can be
That I will always keep with me
A clear sense of CLARITY
That belongs to me

Connections

If we connect the dots
The little circles
The ones that have no end
And no beginning
Because they circle
Around and around

Bring to the surface
What you want to create
Inside the circle of the dot
Find ways to connect them
To make your life strong

Pretend it's a cable
That no one can break
Not even you
Believe in your circle
You connected within
Connect it to something higher
Connect it to God

DISCOVER

I'm arriving
There's no jiving
Over the horizon

In the blink of an eye
You can see the setting sky
That will make you give life a try

By and By
Don't hesitate
To make your point

Everyone has a story
You are not alone
I'm not sure if anyone's perfect
Hope you don't think so
Don't let pride get in your way

So many look down at others
They talk in a flock
There is no need to worry how they mock
For we can all be as sharp as a Hawk

cont.

Really we all stand alone
In the end we all go as one
So let down your defences
Climb your fences
Get out of the old and into the new

DISCOVER your horizon to make a new way
Don't let yesterday get in the way
DISCOVER a brand new way
Starting today

DIVINE TIME

I made the time
I found the time
I created the time
To bring about a newness for me

I was tired of the old
That repeated itself
Over and over again
Like a broken- down record

So I climbed into a new time
That set a new way for me
I never quit believing
Even when I was not achieving

I held on with all my might
Believing time would set me free
A DIVINE TIME
A time of harvest for me
A time for me to believe in me

DRAGONFLY

Transparency within your wings
You fly through the air so gracefully
Legends are told
How you hold
The symbol of renewal and resurrection
After a hardship
Transformation and self realization are also a note
You are known to be free with activity
And carry a spirit with a stiff upper lip
Perhaps you were once a mighty dragon
You are centuries old, and it is known
That you fly about with a sign of harmony
Sometimes you bring light and change in our life
Maybe you're just fun - for you are one

EXPANSION

Like a rubber band
Expand who you are
See Your life
    Your purpose
    Your determination
Grow strong
Release your fears
You held so near
Chaining yourself
Never letting go
Sit quietly
To be one with the ground
Breathe in Breathe out
To settle yourself down
Expand your direction
Like a rubber band
Setting new limits
Breaking free of the old
Stretch your whole being
    Like a cat
    After a nap
Your chance is near
If you hold it dear
To create the EXPANSION
And start a new path

FEATHER IN THE AIR

Let my spirit float free
Like a feather in the air
Sitting in my chair
I can see my spirit carry me
As light as a feather
Floating effortlessly
I give my challenges
To the feather
To take to the air
Floating ever higher
To God above
Trust I must
To let go
As I watch the feather float
Never leaving my chair

GROUNDED

Keep your feet
Solid to the ground
Take off your shoes
And wander around
Release the energies
You don't need
Make it a daily routine

Heart

The light will change
Those HEARTS of dark
It will make a mark
Like a dart
In the HEART
The future is untold
Only our hearts can hold
The changes to unfold
Forget about vanity
Just keep your sanity
In a world gone astray
Stay in the light
To keep your HEART bright

High Vibrations

Vibrations are high within us
All we need comes to us now
We can have peace, we can have calm
The world unwinds, and settles down
The course of the earth is here to learn
Will we be the end of our species?
Will the world evolve by herself?
Keeping nature safe within her
The change of time has begun
Ready I am, I say I am
I will not run or hide
Love I keep within
My soul will flutter like a butterfly
It will fly like an eagle through the sky
Wisdom will direct us
For we live in a world of FAMINE or FEAST
The balance of the spectrum is unselective
Change is inevitable
So give it a try
You can never wonder why
The signs have been by and by
In our hustle and bustle
Everyone missed them
Trying to get to the top
To be the first in line
Instead of Divine

HOLD OUR WORLD DEAR

Hold on tight
With all your might
Say your prayer's everyday
Give gratitude and praise
Along the way
HOLD OUR WORLD DEAR
Everyday
Take away the dark
To bring in the light
Believe that the good
Can defeat the bad
HOLD OUR WORLD DEAR

INNER ME

I have an
        Inner smile
        Inner drive
        Inner determination
        Inner purpose
        Inner love
        Inner acceptance
        Inner light
        Inner fight
        Inner lessons
        Inner creativity
        Inner destination
        Inner faith
        Inner hope
        Inner wisdom
I have an INNER ME!!

KERFUFFLE

There was a KERFUFFLE
That left me all ruffled
I needed to iron it out
To flatten the ruffles
And lose the KERFUFFLE
That scattered me all about

LUMBA

Thanks and praise
To you GOD
In amongst our lives
We all search for treasures
That come from above
Faith comes to life
Mostly when we're in need
Need of a miracle
That will help us be
LUMBA, LUMBA, LUMBA
Thanks and praise
To you GOD
Let us believe
That the treasures
We hold
Are deep inside our souls

MASTERY IN LIFE

Pray, Meditate, Visualize
Find your quiet spot
Stop, be still, listen for awhile
Believe in good
Believe in love
Bring in the light from above
Let God radiate inside
From your head to your toes
Hold on to the feeling
That brings healing
Master your meditation
Say your prayers
Visualize a radiant picture
That makes you feel alive
Bring in some heaven
To make this world better
To make it shine
With God's love
When you work on finding
The MASTERY IN LIFE

MEANING

I'm learning
To find my MEANING
Gleaming through my soul
Teaming with my body and mind
Searching in every hole
Not worrying about a mole
Or a troll to hold me down
Even when life is full of complications
I separate them from trials and tribulations
Making my world full of anticipation
Never letting anyone bring me down
Not even a mole in a hole or a troll
Holding me down
I bring in light, color, a vibration of love to fill me up
Writing like I never wrote before
My pen is my friend
My mind lends me a hand
A force I cannot see accompanies me
Words flow like gold onto my paper
I love what I do and do what I love
Give it a try you all
It's for everyone if you believe
We all have MEANING, deeper than skin
It's all in the soul – for us to hold

Mental Freedom

Take off your mask
That's held you back
Take hold
Never to let go
Find the freedom
In the air
Discover new routes
To be taken
Paths to be walked
Courses to be written
Teachers to teach
To stretch the imagination
Don't let go
Of a freedom you can hold
MENTAL FREEDOM
Build it above you
Build it around you
Build it inside you
Keep it strong
For it is yours
Give it a color
Give it a name
Hold on
To the MENTAL FREEDOM
We all deserve

MY PATH

MY PATH has a reason
I sense a change of season
If I love what I do
I will do what I love
Believing in me
Not worrying about others
Finding the freedom within
Many times I've been let down
Even talked about
There's no use to shout
Or stir about
For if I am patient
The reason will come
To pinpoint my destination
Letting me be me
To set my words free
Creating a PATH
To my destiny

Nobody can be a Somebody

To make you a SOMEBODY
You only have to believe
Everybody can have a
Special way to be a SOMEBODY
TODAY
Little things you do
Changing some of your ways
Can change you from a
Nobody to a SOMEBODY
You only have to believe
Every day Nobody's are doing
Something to be a SOMEBODY today
Believe you are a SOMEBODY
Believe it TODAY

Now

Yesterday became today
There's no way to catch tomorrow
So leave your cares and your worries behind
Learn not to be in a hurry
Take a moment
To find a stillness
Nothing but quiet all around
Portray the now
Find your way how
Your search will fulfill
More than a thrill
It's right here right NOW
Inside your soul
It's better than any trip
You can imagine in the world
So get to the NOW
To find your purpose
It's worth learning how
In the NOW

PEACE AND CALM

PEACE AND CALM surround me now
My focus is clear
Problems in the world
Will disappear
Peace will take time
To find its way to unwind
It's kind of like time
You can't bottle it up
Ideas I inspire
Like a renegade tire
In so many ways
Quit I won't
For I know my boat will float
Easy and relaxed
I write my next quote
I have been here before
I just need a new gear
To put me in overdrive
Over any rocky roads
To smooth out my ride
Using my lessons
To eliminate tension
That I cannot hide
In the fate
That I cannot wait
To anticipate
New ways to be real

PECULIAR

Day turns to night
Night turns to day
This big old world
Has become so challeng'en
The equator is unravel'in
As the poles are unmagnitizen'in
It don't matter who you are
It don't matter what you do
We're all in this together
Our homes are a shift'in
Nobody's gonna be a gift'in
As our world is a drift'in
In PECULIAR ways

Quietness

QUIETNESS surrounds me
I center my soul
My mind is content
Maybe I need to repent
Challenges unfold
Right before me
With the keys I hold
Stories to be told
Work has been done
To prepare for my way
Finding the right outlook
Can be hard to bear
I find my way in quietness
For it gives me strength
To believe in my purpose
Never giving up
Bathing in the goldenness of silence
My mind heals
My body rests
My soul soars
To places a man can't get
QUIETNESS prevails
It makes my heart sing
And brings me to the things
Important to me
Sparks in my soul
Ready to ignite to the light
I bathe in the quiet
That surrounds me so

Reincarnation

Is it real or just in our heads
I always wondered when I went to bed
When I think about it
It hits me like a ton of lead

Who says that being reborn can't be a fact
Something we can't hack
Without making a big chat

I've seen this, I've done this, I've been here before
At times I've been longing for my way back home
Is it a coincidence?
Or could we read into this?
What is real, and what is not?

Maybe a realm of our consciousness
We can recreate - so why may we not
REINCARNATE

Learning our lessons along the way
We may pass or we may fail
We must search for the right trail
To rekindle our spark
We can't let go dark

cont.

Where do the billions upon billions
Of souls of this earth go
Why do we search for other planets on which to live
We surely must learn to give
Give back to earth
To resurrect her

Her water, plants, trees, animals, mammals, insects –
and us
Parasites of people that keep wanting more
Until we burn her to the core

Then we will find out where the billions of souls go
For one day we will all know

SHATTERED

Into a million pieces
Shattered my soul
Fragments of energy
Leaving me cold
To where I don't know

You can't glue them, sew them or mend them
Back together
But with much effort
A transformation can take place
You can heal with grace
To dignify your place

Bringing together the energy
Mends the core
Rebuilding the soul

If you want to maintain your physical body
Remember systems work together on the whole
Body, Mind, and Spirit
We work better when they are together
Paying attention to the direction
We are destined to go

cont.

One foot in front of the other
Just like our thoughts
Portray our attitude
On which way we will go

Pick your destination
To un-shatter the SHATTERED
It's all up to you, to put your pieces together
To gather your resources
And find a new way

Shhhh

Find some time
Just to SHHHH
Bathe in the silence
Let it penetrate to your core
Your body, mind, and soul
Can be of such guidance

If you can SHHHH
Leaving the world behind
Connect your dots
One by one
Bringing in transparency
To let the light flow in

Create your own courses
To help you find the resources
Break down the challenges
One by one
You are the driver
To find your silence within

Discover a world
For only you to find
Your peace, your love, your identity
Where the love and light can flow
So openly, creating silence
With just a SHHHH

Shine and Whine

Don't let go of your shine
And begin to whine
No one wants to listen
When we whine
And don't shine

Silence

The hustle stops the bustle pops
Our chops become still
Nothing is wagered and nothing can be gained
Until we find the goldenness in silence
That will be Heaven on Earth
To stop, take a break, breathe a few breaths
Let your mind take you to places
You'll never get
When you live in a whirlwind
Of chaos and bustle
Always in a hustle
Never coming from within

Spark it Up

In a state of silence, open your mind
SPARK UP THE NEURONS that have been quiet so long
Bring light into darkened areas of your mind
In your state of silence, imagine life turned on

You can push through it – SPARK IT UP
Believe with all your might
That you can bring in the light
Do so in the quietness of your body, mind, and spirit

Believe in the unseen
For miracles have been
Release the past to foresee the future
Don't let people crush your determination

If you can't see it, doesn't mean it's not there
A spark can be invisible
Hidden away
Pray, Meditate, Visualize
With all your might
We are just vessels
Make them shine bright
To be one hell of a sight
Flying as high as a kite
Feeling so light
Like a spark in the night
In the height of your life
Be sure to SPARK UP THE NEURONS
That have been quiet so long

Stepping Stones

First it's one foot
Then the next
Perhaps in a crawl
A walk or run
Building your steps
Anyway that you can
Steps for improvement
Can bring you along
To your destination
To a place you can feel strong
Trust in the process
Leaving your mark
Stones to be stepped on
To make your own trail

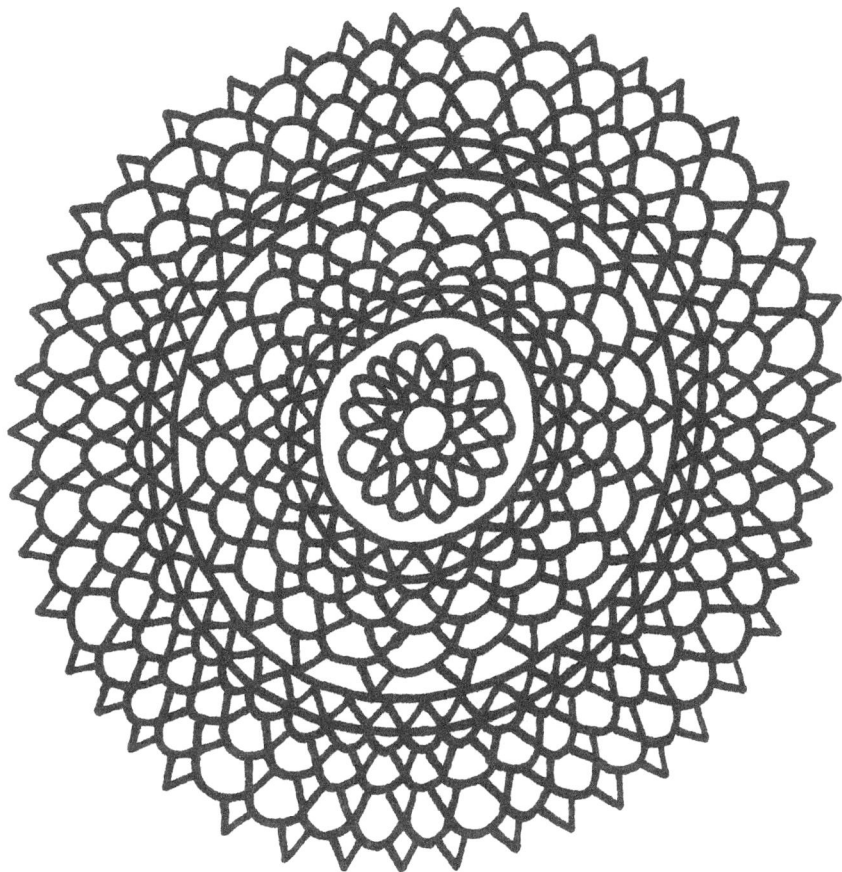

STRETCH YOU MUST

We've lost the MO-JO, there ain't no flow where we go
Our bodies are malfunctioning in so many ways
The only way to stop it is to learn to STRETCH it
If you want to create love inside it don't you hide it

Find what works for you to stretch it
Perhaps it's YOGA
In the downward dog
Maybe it's Tia Chi, Qi Gong, Hanna Somatics, or rolling
on a ball
Down the hall
Don't hit a wall, keep on persisting, not resisting
To find your own routine
Just be sure to find the love everyday
You can change in so many ways

STRETCH your muscles
To stretch your tendons and ligaments
Keep from getting bursitis, tendinitis, or arthritis
That makes you feel OLD
Find the STRETCH and hold it
Bring in the range of motion and flexibility
To the best of your capability

cont.

Remember a little does a lot
Keep those joints lubricated
We don't want them to dry up
STRETCH your core, your limbs, your fingers and toes
Even for a minute or so
Get your hands above your head and reach for the sky
Give it a try

Don't just depend upon massage therapists, chiroprac-
tors, reiki masters
Or energy workers to do the job for you
These are just band-aide solutions, the true magic
comes from within
There is a molecular level to find
Ways to release ourselves
It's just finding the right wave to catch
And how to ride it in

Find the freedom in a STRETCH you can do it almost
anywhere
At home, in the office, at your desk, in a class
The best part it's free
You can learn to lean and lunge
Find your source and make it a course
Make the time to care for yourself
For if you don't no one will for you

cont.

Remove the weights that weigh you down
Bring in a sense of lightness all around
Learn to love to STRETCH inside and out
Pick yourself up to new dimensions
Find a new way of moving and to mention
A new way to relieve tension

STRETCH you can do it standing, sitting, lying
All the while just keep trying
Connect the dots on a cellular level
Break free the damn created within

Find the balance that releasing can bring
It can feel like a million bucks!
Be patient × everything needs time to change
Be kind, take it past your limits within
Your body and mind have a connection
You can make a correction
Learning to renew, restore, and repair the direction
You are destined to go
STRETCH YOU MUST so you don't
Bust and leave behind a trail of rust!

Tension

The TENSION is a wrestling
Messages need attending
Or it will be never ending
The fluctuation is here
Our problems begin within
So don't hesitate
Or it will be to late
If you don't learn how to let go
To heal from the energies
That encircle us so
We tend to bend
Becoming reckless
Hurting our soul
So pick up the pieces
Finding the best way
To pray for a miracle
To unravel the TENSION within

the Course

I needed a new source
So I created a COURSE
It was one of constant discipline
A home study
Is what it was
That I could use as a good resource
To keep me aligned
With the times
A course
To build me up
And make me work on
Believing in a better me
A course
To point me to my destination
Learning new things
To strengthen me
Each and everyday
Through my COURSE

Vibrational Alignment

Nothing is still
From a molecular
Point of view
We are just matter
Atoms and molecules
We as people take up space
Making masses
Not like waves of energy
Like light and sound
Then there are liquids
Like water and ice
They all consist of
VIBRATIONAL ALIGNMENT
To make our world exist

WEE MORNING

It's in the WEE MORNING
The world is unfolding
To produce what this day is holding
Decisions to be made
Games to be played
With new discoveries along the way

In the stillness
Not in the night, nor in the day
In the wee hours
You can pray
To transform your day
When the world is not quite awake

The energies are pure
From the hustle and bustle
Of everyone stirring about
If you catch the peak hours
It's a great place to be
So silent, so still
Are the energies

There can be a reflection and prayer
Bringing a delight to whoever is there
Finding new ways to show you care
In the WEE MORNING

WHEEL OF TIME

The spin begins
The moment conception awakens
You can't see it
But if you pay attention
You can feel it
Like a silent vibration
It's there day and night
The WHEEL OF TIME
May possibly hold our fate
Weak or strong
It's definitely here
Slow or fast
The center is the middle
Where it all begins
The center stays the same
As the spin continues
From the beginning of time
And here after
The WHEEL OF TIME will spin

When No One Believes

I thought it, I wrote it, I spoke it
HELL I even lived it
I climbed the mountainˣ
I made it to the top – my energy radiated
I felt so free I even believed this would be
My lucky breakˣ but it would never be

I picked another mountain, this one had an
extraordinary
Amount of complications to stumble upon
I can make it through this one
I believed with all my might – yet no one believed
As they looked at me with fright

Again & Again & Again I kept trying when I quit
    crying inside
I held my head up high
Or I would never try, for it is not a lie – it is I
My friend said it must surely read upon my headstone
SHE NEVER QUIT TRYING
Even WHEN NO ONE BELIEVED

A man came along that reignited the spark for he
believed
When no one else believed
He let her be she and gave her a key that set her free
WHEN NO ONE BELIEVED

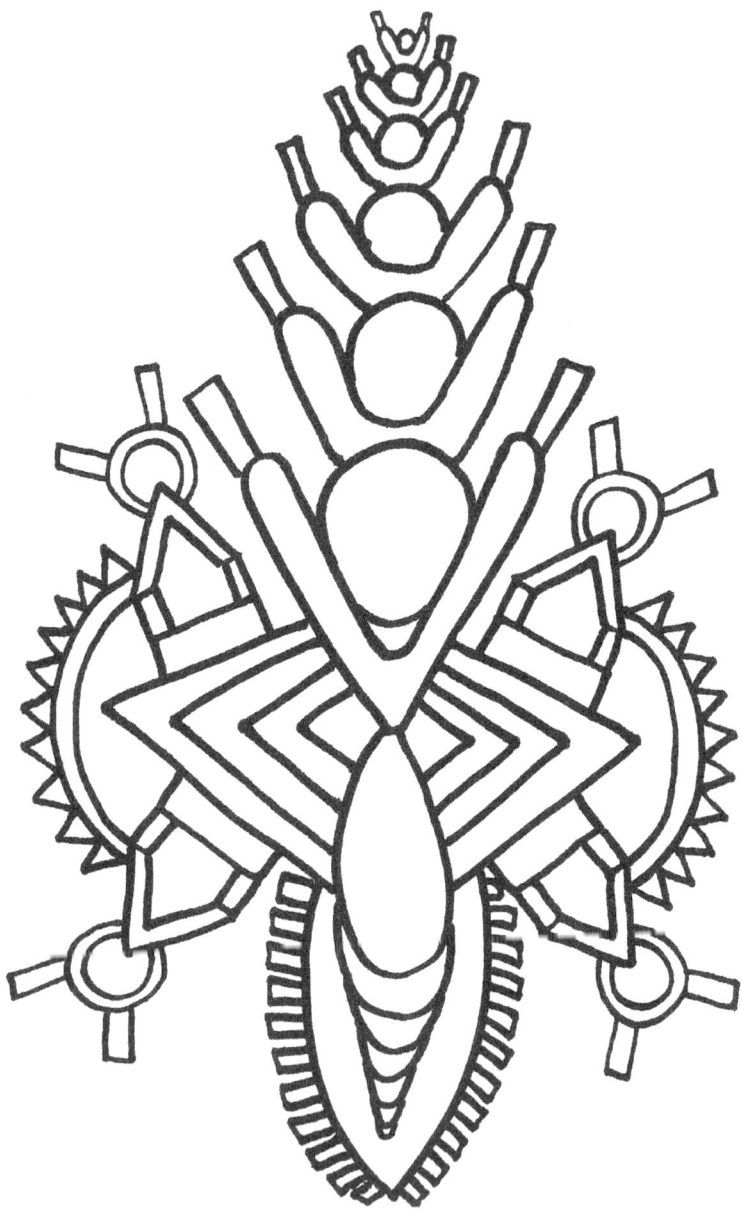

Yesterday's Stones

The glass was crushed
Leaving behind no reminder
Of what it was before

Yesterday was a care away
With nothing left to hold
Just shards of glass
That soon will shape
A new way for today
Restructuring to pave the way
New tales mold the way
Yesterday can't hold you back
Even if the stones are turned
You can shape them in a different way

With the shards of glass
A creation of colors
Is born
Beauty radiates
In such a fine way
Amazing are the structures
Recreated to make today
If you can't get past your past
Take a look at YESTERDAY'S STONES
To recreate your view

Of how yesterday made today
In a beautiful way
And let it all go
To live in the now
Not to recreate your YESTERDAY

Young Whippersnapper

When I was a YOUNG WHIPPERSNAPPER
I Dreamed and Believed
In everything my mind brought to me

When I was a YOUNG WHIPPERSNAPPER
My visions were alive
They brought me hope and color
Keeping me free and alive
As I got older
I began to disbelieve
In my dreams
And what I believed
That kept me free

I faded in color
As hope had become lost
What I believed as a YOUNG WHIPPERSNAPPER
Had left me from my soul

Throughout the decades
I was shredded and cold
Naked and embarrassed
Of who I had become
My dreams had left me
From when I was a YOUNG WHIPPERSNAPPER

cont.

I just needed to believe
To recreate my dreams again
To bring back color
To resurrect myself
Never giving up hope
To transform to what
I was when I was a YOUNG WHIPPERSNAPPER
That made me Dream and Believe

You and Me

I was adrift
When you came along
You put my life into perspective
And helped me to respect it
Intertwined the two of us became one
A loving bond no one can unwind
YOU see ME
And I see YOU
For who we are meant to be

Congratulations on completing *Lumba Poetry: Waves of Change*.

We would love if you could help by posting a review at your book retailer and on the PageMaster Publishing site. It only takes a minute and it would really help others by giving them an idea of your experience.

Thanks

PM Store Author's QR Code
https://pagemasterpublishing.ca/by/barb-flett/

To order more copies of this book, find books by other Canadian authors, or make inquiries about publishing your own book, contact PageMaster at:

PageMaster Publication Services Inc.
11340-120 Street, Edmonton, AB T5G 0W5
books@pagemaster.ca
780-425-9303

catalogue and e-commerce store
PageMasterPublishing.ca/Shop

ABOUT THE AUTHOR

Barb Flett lives in Barrhead, Alberta, Canada with her husband Sheldon. She has a passion for writing and shares some of her trials and tribulations that have made her who she is today. Along with poetry Barb has also spoken to audiences on many aspects of mental illness and how she worked at finding successful recovery. Artwork has been another outlet for her. In 2016 she created two colouring books, XL-erate and Inner Eye Expressions, which are available for sale online.

.